Copyright

Library if Congress Cataloging-in-Publication Data

Burney, Bobby 1963-

Getting to the Truth: Behind the Swamp of Lies

Includes Biblical references from Douay-Rheims Bible revised 1609

Jesus and Mary

Fig. 2 Basilica of the National Shrine of the Immaculate Conception, Washington, DC

Representation of the Holy Son and Mother, Jesus and Mary respectively

Preface

This is an exposition of what is happening in the hearts of those who would destroy America. And a patriotic American's response to that treachery. That treason foisted upon us, the American People, and our Democracy during the 2016 election by the campaign of Donald J. Trump, his more than willing treasonous family members, the Mercers, Cambridge Analytica, the Republican Party. All the congressmen and women who used stolen materials from their fellow Americans. Stolen by the GRU Military Russian officers as well as Cambridge Analytica to advance the Kremlin's cause to destroy Western Europe and the United States of America.

The Kremlin's cause was advanced by Steve Bannon, Roger Stone, Corey Lewandowski, George Papadopoulous, Paul Manafort, Rick Gates, Richard Pinedo, Alex van der Zwaan, Konstantin Kilimnik, George Nadar, Michael Cohen, Michael Flynn, 25 Russian Nationals, (Yevgeny Prigozhin, Mikhail Bystrov, Mikhail Burchik, Aleksandra Krylova, Anna Bogacheva, Sergey Polozov, Maria Bovda, Robert Bovda, Dzheykhun Ogly, Vadim Podkopaev, Gleb Vasilchenko, Irina Kaverzina, and Vladimir Venkov) and Three Russian Companies, (Kremlin's Internet Research Agency, Concord Management and Concord Catering), Vladimir Putin, all those conned into voting for Donald Trump.

Also included are my personal visions of the evil committed by many mentioned in this treatise. I make no excuse for the signs, prophesies, and visions that I have been granted by

Our Lord and Savior Jesus Christ. I share them freely, although they came to me with cost.

The trauma of having to view that which I never wished to see. Throughout this time I learned

the names of the demons and names of the angels of many mentioned in this treatise. As well

as the pet names, some are translated and others are not translated, used by these beings to

refer to those humans used by their demons and those who cooperate with their angels.

Dedicated to the hearts of Jesus and Mary

Fig. 3 Basilica of the National Shrine of the Immaculate Conception, Washington, DC

Representation of the Sacred and Immaculate hearts of Jesus and Mary respectively

O Heart of Jesus pierced for our sins and giving us your Mother on Calvary! O Heart of Mary pierced by sorrow and sharing in the sufferings of your divine Son for our redemption! O sacred union of these Two Hearts! Praised be the God of Love who united them together!

May we unite our hearts and every heart so that all hearts may live in unity in imitation of that sacred unity which exists in these Two Hearts. Triumph, O Sorrowful and Immaculate Heart of Mary! Reign, O Most Sacred Heart of Jesus! – in our hearts, in our homes and families, in the hearts of those who as yet do not know you, and in all nations of the world. Establish in the hearts of all mankind the sovereign triumph and reign of your Two Hearts so that the earth may resound from pole to pole with one cry: Blessed forever be the Most Sacred Heart of Jesus and the Sorrowful and Immaculate Heart of Mary!

Obtain for me a greater purity of heart and a fervent love of the spiritual life. May all my actions be done for the greater glory of God in unions with the divine heart of Jesus and the Immaculate Heart of Mary. Hear and answer our prayers and intentions , save our country from the Kremlin's presidential candidate Donald J. Trump and the Kremlin sponsored religious right, according to your most merciful will. Amen.

Table of Contents

Chapter 1

Fig. 4 Basilica of the National Shrine of the Immaculate Conception, Washington, DC
Representation of Our Lord crucified for our sins.

Thou shalt have no other gods before me

(Exodus Chapter 20 verse 3)

The hand of the Kremlin can be seen in the daily disruption of American political life since the 2016 election. Even if the Divider-n-Chief, Donald J. Trump, calls Vladimir Putin we Americans only hear about it from the Kremlin news source, TASS. We never hear it from this traitorous White House. This should give pause to any patriotic American!

The Divided States of America is compromised by the illegitimate infestation in the White House, Donald J. Trump. He inflicts his demonic criticism against all patriotic Americans regarding his compromised relationship to the Kremlin. Despite the overwhelming avalanche of reports of the tsunami of evidence of Kremlin espionage, kompromat, and indicted criminals. Congressional and Senate leadership is absolutely silent and have done nothing to protect Americans from past Kremlin past cyber attacks and less than nothing to protect Americans from future attacks. With Donald J. Trump leading the way as the puppet of the Kremlin leaving us and our allies open to further attacks with no defense or offense being prepared. Pope Francis," Umm-ah-kha-aula, his guardian angel's name for him" declares the master / slave relationship between the Kremlin and this illegitimate administration "dangerous."

Donald J. Trump prepares for his further instruction and indoctrination from his Kremlin handlers calling it a summit. His attempt to thaw relations with the Kremlin by his secret calls from the White House which we as Americans only found out about by the Kremlin's' gracious press. This plan which is in your face obvious and has no American or allied upside to it, just like the summit with Kim Jong Un. This plan which is to break up the EU, NATO and NAFTA as well as any other positive relationship we had in the world is blessed by a seemingly unusual source: Franklin Graham, a prominent member of the Religious Right and the son of deceased evangelist Billy Graham. This is done as a slap in the face to all patriotic God-fearing moral Americans. The younger Grahama longtime Trump stooge lead a prayer, to whom I do not know, at the president's inauguration. He published a Facebook posting voicing optimism about Trump-Kremlin partnership.

Franklin states, "The media and enemies of President Trump," (i.e. true American Patriots), "have tried to drive a wedge between Russia and the United States, Our country needs Russia as an ally in the fight against Islamic terrorism. Join me in praying for President Trump and President Vladimir Putin as they have this very strategic meeting." What is particularly striking is the demonic image which is painted by this man is exactly what Satan or the Kremlin would say.

How are the three so closely aligned? Here is a blatant and malicious attack against the free press the cornerstone of any liberal democracy. United States of America is a liberal constitutional democracy! If you want to live in a conservative constitutional democracy then move to Russia, (2010 the highest number of abortions per woman of child bearing age of any country in the world and the USSR from 1920 allowed abortion for any reason at anytime during pregnancy), but leave your, protests against abortion, business interests, bibles, guns, and freedoms here. You will not find the government there very open to your way of life.

A so-called religious leader heaping praise on a Kremlin-Trump master-slave relationship may surprise some, but this man's post belies a deeper conspiracy that is already shaping American politics. Franklin, working under the auspices and rule of the Kremlin's church officials and select few of his compromised colleagues, has already pledged allegiance to the Kremlin which continues to use false faith and kompromat as tools to accrue power. How do the so-called religious bind themselves to common criminals and murderers like Donald J. Trump and the Kremlin? Where does this moral corruption have its roots?

Russia is not a bastion of religious freedom. The 2018 U.S. Commission on International Religious Freedom report listed the country as one with a worsening repressive record in religious freedom, pointing to policies that limit the activities of Muslims and other minority religious groups such as Jehovah's Witnesses and Pentecostals especially in the illegally annexed Crimea. To all of this Donald J. Trump and Franklin Graham turn a blind eye giving their Kremlin handlers mulligan after mulligan.

Yet Franklin Graham's remarks are the result of a years-long recruitment effort by the Kremlin, which is well known for using faith—particularly the Russian Orthodox Church, whose reach extends beyond Russian borders—as a mechanism to expand its country's influence and antagonize Western opponents. The white evangelical as well as their Kremlin handlers' agenda of hate is modeled on the Kremlin's unrestrained lust for dominance over Western Democracies. And both their own realizations that their message is unpalatable, destructive and completely unchristian.   They have decided that an unholy alliance is their best form for survival. This is best exemplified in the Star Wars movie when the Emperor reveals his true nature in the Senate and they kowtow rather than fight against him.

The unchristian and unholy evangelicals who by their own admission do not evangelize find their influence and their numbers dwindling. As Christ said the truth is not to be found in them. These white washed sepulchers who rather support anarchist autocrats who are murderers, racists, misogynists, and all around negative creeps. Whose place in hell I have been given a vision which I will share with you.

As my guardian angel guides my feet along a barren field where there is no life, mineral, microbial, vegetative, or animal. Yet all around me are the whispers of the damned denizens. I cannot make out what they are saying but the sound of hushed curses and sick wailing of self-inflicted contamination. The place descends lower and lowers and becomes dimmer as shadows of misshapen beings pushes in all around me. The heat, the stench, the dimmed vision and the hushed guttural whispers calling for me to join them cause me to retch, cough, and choke. I do not know how much of this I can endure as time seems to have no meaning here as nothing changes only the oppressive encroaching voices grow into a rising crescendo, cacophony, and claustrophobic din.

Now I see clearly as my guardian angel pulls me back to the heavenly light away from this self imposed nonsense. The key for each being to this prison of living death is found within as its gates can only be opened from the inside.

I care little for what denomination you belong or whether you are an atheist or agnostic or uninterested in you final end. My only reason to write this treatise on the demonic forces that rule leaders around the world; it is the reason I was I was placed on this planet. Every lesson that I have learned has lead me to write this treatise and to expose the nonsense that we are experiencing and to illuminate the path forward. Many reading this will be offended by the comparing of white evangelicals to the Sadducees and Pharisees at the time of Jesus Christ.

Others will cry out in favor of this idea while I may not agree with either so let me underscore who I mean in this exposition. If you belong to a sect that supported human slavery in any form this is being addressed to you. If you belong to a sect that spends a huge amount of time and effort excoriating the sexually crippled this is aimed directly at you. Transgender, gay, queer, lesbian people will never tell you that their nature lends to the pinnacle of human sexuality which results in human life. Like a cripple man will never tell you that the paralysis he experiences will lead to athletic super human speed. But we do not judge the cripple as being less than you human and deserving the mindless hated espoused by the Kremlin and the white evangelicals.

Franklin Graham homosexuals are not mentioned in the ten commandments or the two great commandments of love and the Roman Centurion who pleaded for the life of his lover/slave was professed to have greater faith than anyone in Israel. Apparently much greater faith than you Franklin Graham, Urka-Shi-'ah-'hah meaning "you white washed sepulcher!" Your demon Beelzebub's pet name for you not mine.

Black Americans have understood the scourge of white evangelicals and their special place in Hell more than any people on this planet. They could not in good conscience vote for a pedophile or a lech for US Senate and US President respectively, both who support Vladimir Putin. The truth is you are know by your works not what you believe. Which is the expression of the content of your character; how you ACT!

White evangelicals with their deep roots in misogyny, racism, human slavery, and white supremacist movements bent on unwinding protections for women and minorities the world over have increasingly leaned on the Kremlin model for direction and support. Targeting as does the Kremlin repression of women, any minority group, and LGBTQ people their families and friends to undoing their rights throughout the world.

The foulest examples who have the lowest levels of hell reserved for them are Rick Joyner, Ken Ham, Jeff Sessions, Jim Jordan, Stephen Miller, Devin Nunes, Roy Cohen, Michelle Bachmann, Arthur Jones, Donald J. Trump, Jerry Falwell Jr. and Sr., Richard Spenser, Sean Donahue, Joe Abarr, Tom Tancredo, Roger Ailes, Sean Hannity, Joe Arpaio, Augustus Invictus aka Austin Gillespie, Paul Nehlen, Lou Barletta, Mitch McConnell, Paul Ryan, James Dobson, Steve King, Matt Gaetz, Corey Stewart, Dana Rohrabacher, Steve Bannon, Tony Suarez, Franklin Graham, David Duke, Richard Land. I will describe through out the book in as much detail as is afforded me the place in hell that they themselves have prepared for all eternity as well as their ancestors who call to them in the din of despair.

This is the first of two visions I had of the Trump's Family in Hell. January 27th 2017 my Guardian Angel and I descended into hell and I was brought into a Cave like structure with Freddy Trump Jr. there screaming out Donald J. Trump's name. There was also a serpent like figure with a somewhat misshapen human head which gave off an horrific odor and caused my skin to crawl. I immediately knew it was Roy Cohen. Without a mouth, he was wailing out Donald J. Trump's name. I awoke from this vision and immediately prayed to God as I smelled an acrid smoke found burn holes in my bed sheets. Later did I read an article and found out that Donald had a brother named Freddy. I already knew the sad history of the demonic fiend who is Roy Cohen. The smell of his stench will never leave me. He did not speak to me or even recognize that I was there. Thanks be to God.

The political benefits of this most unholy union for the Kremlin are obvious. The Religious Right would be an easy prize for anyone looking to gain influence in American politics by spreading hatred. White Evangelical Christianityhave long played an active role in elections especially espousing hatred for anyone who looks or acts differently. If there are any White Evangelicals reading this book from the seminary to the pew who disagree with me then my your life prove me wrong! What's more, some of their most controversial including Franklin Graham have only gained influence during the madness of Trump's rise to the national stage. The alignment between some American hate sponsoring religious conservatives and their Kremlin handlers predate Donald J. Trump.

Trump is creating a new form of Christian nationalism centered on himself but the shift has accelerated in recent years. This violates the first commandment and assures the befouling curse that those who commit this insanity that they will become like the idol they worship. The vision I have had of Senator John Sidney McCain III final end with all of the rejoicing in heaven is juxtaposed against the sad final end to the Trump and his ilk.

The phrase "in God we trust" was added to US currency on July 30th 1956. According to the legislation of 1954 "under God" was inserted into the Pledge of Allegiance in an effort to distance America from Russia's officially officially atheistic disposition. In 1943 the united States Supreme Court ruled that no person can be required to recite the pledge. Thou shalt have no other gods before Me!

Chapter 2

Fig. 5 Basilica of the National Shrine of the Immaculate Conception, Washington, DC Representation of Our Lady and Our Lord.

Thou shalt not make idols

(Exodus Chapter 20 verse 4)

Thou shalt not make to thyself a graven thing, nor the likeness of any thing that is in heaven above, or the earth beneath, nor of those things that are in the waters under the earth.

Donald J. Trump has spent decades erecting idols to himself. Both in the metaphorical sense as well as in the physical sense he is the arch-type of an idolater. Many people miss the point in idolatry which is the worship of that which by nature and essence is lower than you which is an insult to humanity as well as to the One True God.   With his grandfather's fake name emblazoned on every building he builds and ornament he resells reminds all who see it what Donald J. Trump thinks of himself.

And most importantly what he thinks of them. He sees himself as, "el muy muy". A Spanish colloquialism which means a 'the bad ass' who incorrectly thinks he knows best usually in those areas where he knows nothing or very little.

This is why he has to lie about his accomplishments all of the time because they are non-existent. What could that possibly mean that the emperor has no clothes? Then what does that say about his sycophants, devoted followers, and ass-kissers? He believes that he is "the best president that God ever created," "the most militaristic person ever," "the best negotiator," "the best wall builder," and having "the best words." Trump worships himself and demands that others put him on a pedestal and treat him with the reverence due to gods and

kings – of which he is neither. This is a trait of all boorish autocrats.

Chapter 3

Fig. 6 Basilica of the National Shrine of the Immaculate Conception, Washington, DC Representation of Our Lady welcoming all her children.

Thou shalt not take the name of the Lord in vain

(Exodus Chapter 20 verse 7)

Thou shalt not take the name of the Lord thy God in vain: for the Lord shall not hold him guiltless that shall take the name of the Lord God in vain.

What is the practice of the Old Testament required of humanity to honor God's great power and might by imitation? "What does the Lord require so that you do not misuse or take His Name in vain? All that is required:" To do justice, and to love kindness, and to walk humbly with your God."

To do justice. Stealing an election by taking money and ill-gotten secrets from a foreign enemy defying the law of the land and using foreigners to promote your campaign is not just or correct. Stealing a fair days wage from workers and contractors is not just. Proposing racist and misogynistic laws to hurt your fellow citizens is not just. Proposing harsher sentences so that you can fill more jail space because builders of jails supported your bid for presidency is not just. Lying endlessly as your Kremlin handlers tell you to do is not just. Tearing down the alliances of the west and starting trade wars uselessly and praising all enemies of truth, justice and the democratic way. None of these support human or divine justice.

Donald Trump does not love human or christian kindness. In none of his hellish rhetoric about hurting others who oppose him during and after his campaign reflects kindness in even the most remote definition of the word. Children that you ignored along with their mothers and saying that you support the rights of the unborn while stomping on the rights of the born. This reflects nothing of kindness. Stirring up tensions between different groups within your own country let alone your own political party. One whose sole purpose is to sow discord among brothers such as, Donald J. Trump, Stephen Miller, and Jeff Sessions. This points to nothing even close to the true meaning of human let alone christian kindness. The worst parts of Hell are reserved for those who accomplish this discord. I will describe that scene below.

May 18th 2017 I awoke with a start after a terrible dream. It was of a hideous creature that had been named Roger Ailes. It plummeted to the bowels of hell like a streak of darkness and mendacity against the light of the morning sky. Screaming aloud the name of Donald J. Trump. He landed in a dark hole where strange sounds were belching forth from the beneath him. He kept screaming out No, no, n…. It was horrifying as he was transformed what he had become on earth. The description is almost caused me to vomit but I awoke instead.

And finally walking humbly and with proper deference with our God. Bowing to the will of your Kremlin atheistic handlers is not an example of walking humbly at all. Claiming that you are the leader of only some Americans and not all. The failure in all three, to do justice, to do kindness and to walk humbly with God, brings disrespect upon God's character and abuses His Holy Name. God please deliver us from this abomination!

Chapter 4

Fig. 7 Basilica of the National Shrine of the Immaculate Conception, Washington, DC
Representation of Our Lady and Our Lord with the Rosary in mosaic.

Thou shalt keep holy the sabbath
(Exodus Chapter 20 verse 8)

Donald J. Trump has never been known to go to church unless he found it expedient for some other end or to be seen. Mar-a-Lago is not a church or even a meeting of God-fearing folks but like the merchants in the temple is a place where money and power are the true gods. One cannot serve both God and mammon.

Remembering the Sabbath each weak has never been more important that it is in this fast paced, helter-skelter, demeaning world in which we live. It has always been, as the commandment teaches, about sanctifying a day so that we may remember that God alone deserves our love and devotion. And that sorrow for our sins and true repentance is what brings sanctity to every day.

Chapter 5

Fig. 8 Basilica of the National Shrine of the Immaculate Conception Icon of Ichthus as the Alpha and the Omega. Jesus Christ Son of the Living God The Beginning and the End.

Thou shalt honor thy parents

(Exodus Chapter 20 verse 12)

Honor thy father and thy mother, that thou mayest be long lived upon the land which the Lord thy God will give thee. This is a commandment that comes with a promise associated with it.

Donald J. Trump's mother, Mary Anne MacLeod, was born in Scotland in 1912. On February 17, 1930 she was issued an immigration visa. On May 2, 1930, MacLeod departed Glasgow on board the RMS *Transylvania* arriving in New York City on May 11, 1930. Like many immigrants, she dreamed of becoming a US citizen. She began working as a domestic servant and was naturalized twelve years later on March 10, 1942.

Donald J. Trump's Muslim ban and orders to the border patrol and ICE to kidnap children from their parents and then secret them off into orphanages in the middle of the night with no plan to reunite them. These prove beyond a shadow of a doubt that he has no respect for the family.

This should be of no surprise as he ignored all of his children until they were useful to him. He has ignored, cheated on and abused all of his wives as well as hundreds of other women. This is on video tape with the apprentice and his access holly wood video tape as well as in sealed court records. This is truly a demon in human flesh. He has no respect for families or family values nor does he have christian moral values. May God bless you

Melania Trump for all that you have suffered! There may not be enough holy water in the world to wash the stench of him off of you. I fear for you and pray for you that you may walk away from that abusive relationship. No one deserves to be treated as poorly as you are.

Using children to hide behind his immoral immigration policies is the clearest sign of his abysmal moral dereliction. Immigration security problems that he perceives; were not the issue with his Mother or his current wife. But somehow they are if the woman's name is Maria. Then she deserves to be hurt, humiliated and treated like dirt before her babies are ripped from her and she is jailed by Donald J. Trump.

Second vision of Trump's family in hell. On the morning of May 18, 2017 I saw Roger Ailes descend down to the same hellish cave-like structure screaming out Donald J. Trump's name. Later that day I would have to look up this person only to find out that he had died and left a legacy of lechery and misogynistic filth. Then I saw Freddy Trump Jr.

I asked Freddy Trump if any other Trump members were with him. Without answering three figures came out from the shadows. Freddy Trump Sr., his wife and a small little girl steeped forward. They made no sign of happiness, or noise or calling Donald's name. Only that they came together and were promptly dismissed and receded into the shadows from whence they had appeared. Their three faces were all malformed and misshapen. I will leave that image alone as I have already described it in detail in a White House email. For which I received a prompt thank you. Truly no one in the White House has eyes or can read English.

Chapter 6

Fig. 9 Basilica of the National Shrine of the Immaculate Conception, Washington, DC
Representation of Nuestra Senora de Caridad, Our Lady of Charity.

Thou shalt not kill

(Exodus Chapter 20 verse 13)

Donald J. Trump's failure to deliver aid in Puerto Rico places the blood of almost 5000 souls on his small hands. Placing a murderer as head of the EPA, Scott Pruitt was found to be a liar when the Oklahoma courts realized that he with his lawyer friends decided from the internet what drugs to use to kill prisoners. The blood of Clayton Lockett and Charles Warner screams from the earth and God has heard their cries for vengeance just as he had heard their calls for forgiveness.

Trump calls to his supporters to harm others that disagree with him. He heaps praise on Dictators and murderers like Vladimir Putin and offends our allies and friends at every chance he gets. World War III will be caused by Donald J. Trump and his co-conspirators in Congress. Their lack of article two oversight is a grave disservice to the Americans that they expect to protect their useless asses in an armed conflict.

On the topic of Abortion it is my firm belief that whether a human being is one cell or six trillion cells he / she is a human being. I firmly believe that respect needs to be paid regardless of development or age. Now that being said this man holds human life in the lowest possible estimation. He cares nothing about the rights of the unborn unless it could buy him the votes of the born. No human could care about mothers or their children and then vote against universal healthcare. This demon never hides his disdain for human life. He has promoted the ideas of denying women healthcare as well as their unborn, jailing their children

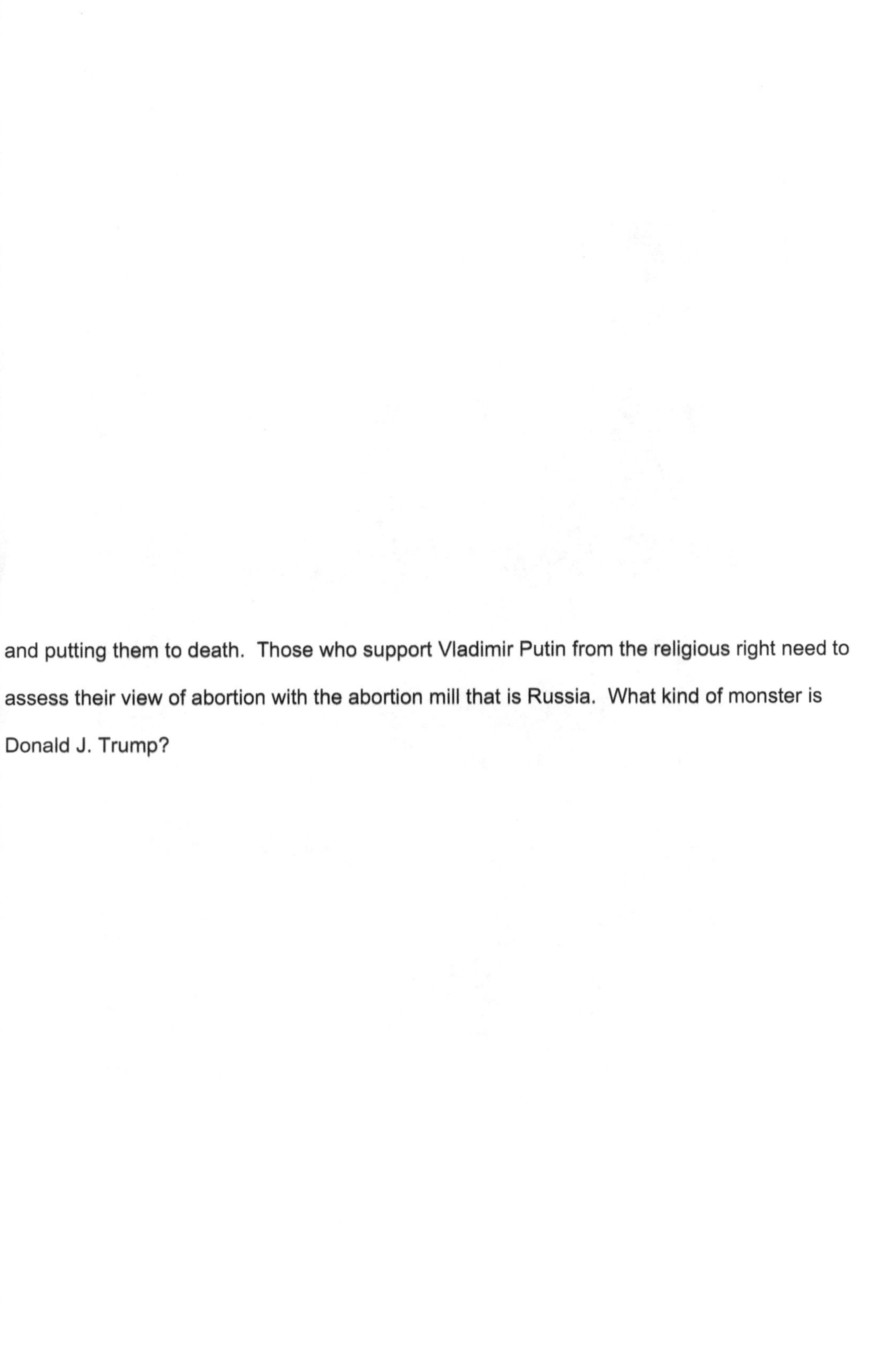

and putting them to death. Those who support Vladimir Putin from the religious right need to assess their view of abortion with the abortion mill that is Russia. What kind of monster is Donald J. Trump?

Chapter 7

Fig. 10 Basilica of the National Shrine of the Immaculate Conception, Washington, DC

Representation of Nuestra Senora de Guadalupe, Our Lady of Guadalupe.

Thou shalt not commit adultery

(Exodus Chapter 20 verse 14)

Donald J. Trump does not respect women and is not a role model for young boys or husbands. He has three failed marriages. There is a prophesy if you can read. Melania you are free and do not need his abuse. You are beautiful and there is a man you currently know who would love and cherish you as you and your son deserve. You know in your sweet soul what God's will for you. It is not that piping hot mess. May God bless you my friend and my sister.

Stormy Daniels we know you love your country. Prophesy your daughter has in her to become a very saintly nun, do not fight what God has begun in her. Michael Avenatti you are a hero in this fight against the moral turpitude of Donald j. Trump. Karen McDougal will be there to denounce how she was used by Donald J. Trump. For all of the times Donald J. Trump has seemed pleased, no proud, of his marital infidelity and blatantly sexist tendencies. Many white males identify with this sickness. Assuming it is some sign of virility when in actuality it is a pseudo virility and false manliness. Being a man-whore is not an ideal that anyone should be trying to achieve. Even the words turn into acid in one's mouth. The very opposite is the truth in fact it is a pit of self-destruction and perversity which destroys all that it is around it.

Chapter 8

Fig. 11 Basilica of the National Shrine of the Immaculate Conception, Washington, DC
Representation of of Titan's Assumption of the Blessed Virgin Mary.

Thou shalt not steal

(Exodus Chapter 20 verse 15)

Donald Trump's charitable foundation had received many millions in donations only to be stolen and misappropriated by the Donald J. Trump. Donald J. Trump's school which stole millions from hard working Americans. He made a campaign donation to a morally corrupt state Attorney General and she invalidated many more claims to steal American's due process and justice.

Using Kremlin sponsored methods against the Republican front runners in the elections to beat them and steal the Republican Nomination. While Paul Manafort reported to his Russian handlers of his ability to manipulate the Republican platform and destroy the Republican party from the inside. All of this in plain site to the applause of white evangelicals. Even they should understand thou shalt not steal!

But most upsetting is his current attempt to steal away the US good will and leadership in the world as well as the soul of our democracy. For this he shall fall and in the worse possible way (prophesy).

Chapter 9

Fig. 12 Basilica of the National Shrine of the Immaculate Conception, Washington, DC
Representation of of Murillo's Immaculate Conception of the Blessed Virgin Mary..

Thou shalt not commit perjury

(Exodus Chapter 20 verse 16)

(Thou shalt not bear false witness against thy neighbor.)

2016 United States of America Presidential Election was subverted by the Republican Candidate Donald J. Trump. It was a coordinated conspiracy to defraud the American People by the Trump campaign and the Kremlin. Donald J. Trump is the first puppet American President of Vladimir Putin's Russian Kleptocracy. Donald's compromising relationship with the Kremlin / Russian Mob and his continuous lying to the American People has led us to the Divided States of America.

Eighth or Ninth Commandment: "You shall not bear false witness against your neighbor." Donald J. Trump is a pathological liar or competitor to Satan who is the father of lies. "When he lies, he speaks his native language, for he is a liar and the father of lies." (John 8:44) Today, our culture maintains a distinction between lying versus perjury. Biblical texts point to a similar a distinction between lying in general and bearing false witness, perjury. On the one hand, bearing false witness, perjury, that was always prohibited according to the ten commandments. Lying in general was acknowledged to be, in certain circumstances "permissible or even commendable", when it was not under oath and it was not harmful to others.

We find ourselves in a world where the Illegitimate president of the Divided States of America who also is the author of the Divided Nations embodies completely what the proverbs writer found abominable in the face of God. "There are six things that the Lord hates, seven that are an abomination to him: haughty eyes, a lying tongue, and hands that shed innocent blood, a heart that devises wicked plans, feet that make haste to run to evil, a false witness who breathes out lies, and one who sows discord among brothers."[1]

The first abomination is pride. Haughty eyes, pride, hubris the primal sin of Satan whether it shows itself as sexism, racism, nationalism or any of the other isms that are piled upon the dunghill of human tragedy and failed ideologies. Why would patriotic Americans vote into office a perjurer with an ideology that is expressly made to divide and conquer? Why would patriotic Americans vote into office someone whose vile, voracious, and bottomless appetite for human vanity and self praise would allow him to say or do anything?

The second abomination is a lying tongue. Why would the externally religious and externally patriotic flock to someone who spews forth the venom of Satan? Why would the externally religious and externally patriotic flock to someone who invites as advisers those mentally weak, irreligious, unpatriotic, divisive, and avid liars? According to the voting patterns of most true Americans and the resultant resistance after the election most true Americans would not. In the "Divided States of America" or "Trumpistan" as we lay under the divider-n-liar Donald J. Trump.

The third abomination are hands that shed innocent blood. The lackluster response to the hurricane Maria killing almost 5,000 Americans in Puerto Rico. The Opiod crisis for which

---

1   . ^ Proverbs 6:16-19 English Standard Version (ESV)

the President has taken money away and reneged on his promise to do anything substantial against it. Instead of talking about the Post Offices' response to the crisis he has wasted both the American people's and the Postmaster General's time talking about raising prices to hurt Amazon and ultimately the American people.   The healthcare attack to strip away the chance for affordable health for millions. Those deaths are on his bloodied hands. This is exactly what Vladimir Putin had in mind in throwing support behind this demonic person.

The fourth abomination is a heart that devises wicked plans. The list of racist, sexist, and hate mongering statements of one group of Americans against the another cascades from the heart of this vile criminal in torrents. He is literally a fire hose of abominable ideological filth. Much like his Kremlin handlers who rejoice every time that his mouth or twitter spew forth the filth that infests his small lifeless heart. His diabolical rhetoric which he mimics from the hypocritical, lying, self-loathing homosexual jew, Stephen Miller. Who in Nazis Germany would have felt quite at home as a German bar of soap.

The fifth abomination are feet that that make haste to run to evil.   The list of immediate knee-jerk responses from the Muslim travel ban to the moving of the embassy to Jerusalem. The city of peace? Healthcare that he wanted to strip away. Foolishly running into a meeting with Kim Jong Un or Vladimir Putin to give a dictator a ridiculous amount of praise and other giveaways with nothing in return. Rushing to have a tryst with White House, this is for what? The troops he sent against us in Syria. For support of Iran? What love fest will these two sickos pull off. The demons in Hell howl with unmitigated and unbridled lust. Pulling us out of

TPP, Paris Accord, Iran deal, G7, and the UN Human Rights group. This sent Satan into an all out victory lap but he was beaten to that only by White House.

The sixth abomination is a false witness that breathes out lies. The list is almost endless but apparently since like his father his native tongue is lying. What base supports the fire hydrant of lies? The active measure of the Kremlin. That is one of their primal directives. Lie endlessly about everything so as to lull your listeners into a stupefied trance.

The seventh is one who sows discord among brothers. This list writes itself on a daily basis. Donald J. Trump's constant demonic attacks on our NATO Allies or on our American States Allies or on our Asian Allies or on his republican allies or on our fellow Americans which has created the Divided States of America. The Divided Nations. His attacks on the EU by illegal trade tariffs is exactly what his Kremlin handlers want him to do. This needs to be kept in mind but just laugh at this buffoon and conman as well as those he has conned. We all know their moment of realization will be horrific and they will need our laughter to heal them. To heal our democracy and civil society.

Chapter 10

Fig. 13 Basilica of the National Shrine of the Immaculate Conception, Washington, DC
Representation of the Miraculous Medal of the Blessed Virgin Mary.

Thou shalt not covet

(Exodus Chapter 20 verse 17)

Thou shall not covet thy neighbor's house: neither shalt thou desire his wife, nor his servant, nor his handmaid, nor his ox, nor his ass, nor any thing that is his.

Donald J. Trump has openly coveted that he had the inauguration of Barack Obama. He has openly coveted millions of people rallying, marching and resisting across the country and around the world. He has openly coveted overwhelming popularity. Donald J. Trump has openly coveted the popular vote.

Donald J. Trump openly covets attention of the North Koreans to Kim Jong Un, the Military parades of Europe and Asia, fading glory of demeaning your opponents with your own vices, Dictators Cruel and Barbaric lust for power and Victory at all costs. Donald J. Trump openly covets his neighbor's whatever. He is not even bright enough to see the huge error of his ways.

Sorry Donald J. Trump and his cohort of liars: President Barack Obama holds the record for the biggest inauguration crowd in history, your approval ratings are lower than the percentage of those who believe you should be impeached for defrauding the American people. Secretary Hillary Clinton did win the popular vote. Yes a woman beat you without having to cheat and defraud the American people or invite the Kremlin's bots to do his dirty work. You will never get what you want. Because not sex, money, adulation or insane lying will ever fill the ever widening hole that is in your soul.

Let me describe in detail this lecherous, deviant, greedy soul that I see before my mind's eye. This is a soul who is so putrid and undeveloped in true human virtue that it is left only with its negative biting criticism of all that is good. These negative verbal attacks only affect those souls with its disease of damnation. So as to deny any good to the future of others and only pestilence and death live in its touch. It wants to deny any good in the future as it sees its own future bereft of good.

Vision three: Donald J. Trump is in the Rose Garden and is announcing the end of America's participation in the Paris accord. The face of Donald J. Trump looks as if something red covered it briefly. It is the super imposed face of Loki who was given free reign of Donald J. Trump by the Don himself.

Vision four: The above sight is repeated when the announcement came that the American embassy would be moved to Jerusalem. Many see it as a speech impairment but what I saw was Loki contorting Donald's face into the future misshapen creature that he is on the fast track to become.

Fig. 14 Basilica of the National Shrine of the Immaculate Conception, Washington, DC Representation of Our Lord on the Cross.

The Axis of Evil

(Mitch McConnell, Paul Ryan, & Donald J. Trump)

Mitch McConnell

Where do you think Trump learned to gaslight America? Gaslighting is a form of psychological manipulation that seeks to sow seeds of doubt in a targeted individual or in members of a targeted group, making them question their own memory, perception, and sanity.

All of the constant frustrations that we have to deal with in these Divided States of America is the fear mongering and the lie driven hysteria. The obsession with misreporting the news by media giant Fox News whose reputation for misrepresentation is enormous. Add to that Sinclair News agency which is in league with Satan to doom the American democratic experience and fully indoctrinate its viewers with prime-time slime Trumpism.

With all sincerity that Trump represents a danger to our country, our moral identity, our democracy, our sense of decency, our world. This is clear from every Washington Post, Daily Beast, New York Times article and the fear felt in every announcement on breaking news. As the free press does an outstanding join of informing the populace and representing our concerns and questions. We find in the macro world what I found in mine own. I was born and raised in Washington, DC the city known for never having voted for a criminal for President. DC voted 90% against Donald J. Trump. It is an occupational /

residential hazard that the nation votes in assholes and we are forced to live with them. I

decided that taxation without representation was outrageous so I moved to Texas and got the

same deal.

When I met Senators Rafael Cruz and John Cornyn who both could care less what the

voters say. Also Representative John Culberson who was so distasteful and rude in his

responses that I had to move from his district because they all forgot what it means to be a

public servant. In fact outside the office of John Cornyn I was threatened by one of his

staffers because I accidentally touched his arm. We know all of the scandals of these so

called public servants. While some of us have been given the names of their demons and the

demons' names for them. This is a most uncomfortable gift but its burden does have a bright

spot. You can command them to do your bidding with this knowledge but I must warn you that

you must be a holy person or you might find your self obsessed or worse possessed. Please

handle this information with holy water and a holy life. This is not true of the angelic names

and the names of their angels.

This brings us to Mitch McConnell. I am not exaggerating when I say that Mitch

McConnell is evil. The Donald J. Trump has already an assembled a line of shitty demonic

cabinet that hold no love for their country. The fact that Mitch McConnell, Urka-Shia-Shuh as

he is known by Moloch, now holds near-total power over the Senate is perhaps the most

unbearable sideshow in The Axis of Evil. Here is a man who made it his solemn oath not to

uphold the constitution but to obstruct justice and assist the Kremlin. McConnell is the evil

man who hijacked a Supreme Court vacancy with lies, deceptions and changing the rules for

Donald J. Trump, refused to allow the American people to know that the Kremlin was behind the Trump campaign. Donald J. Trump hates Mitch McConnell's guts just as Loki hates Moloch.

Now we find out that McConnell is basically a traitor for no other reason than to screw over the American People. Contrast Mitch to John McCain whose angle is Azreal and whose angelic name is Umm-lee-ahl.

Vision: I see John standing in light surrounded by the love of Jesus Christ with his guardian angel watching over that part of creation for which he commands dominion. His entrance into Heaven is glorious and earth shattering. He teaches us the most important lesson. Laugh at your enemies for like Donald J. Trump their end will be hysterical. As they thought of themselves little gods and found in the end how little they matter.

Mitch McConnell's did get his wife a Cabinet post. This man has no morals, nor any respect for the rule of law, nor any respect for those who voted for him. As Chinese, Europeans, Canadians and Asians levy tariffs against industries in his state he stands by and does nothing. Are you seeing a pattern?   For his own personal gain, he permitted the Kremlin to continue manipulating the American people so that his party's candidate could win and his wife would get a Cabinet position. Giving the American people that evil illegitimate infestation in the White House.

This is treason, giving comfort to an adversary while we are under attack. Just because you do not hear the bombs dropping from the sky right now does not mean we are not being softened up for World War III. After the summit with Putin you can be assured that Donald J. Trump would sell all NATO and US secrets for a Russian Trump Tower while American children die in a war he set the ground work for us to lose. There's no other way to put this more clearly Donald J. Trump and Mitch McConnell chose the Kremlin over and the Divided States of America over the constitution and the United States of America. They should be prosecuted and tried for high treason.   Unless we hold them accountable in the for their crimes against our nation we stand as complicit criminals with them.

Mitch has been saying for decades along with the his stooges at Fox News and Sinclair Broadcasting that the dangers of his so-called political opponents would play into the hands of the real adversaries of the U.S.A. This has only to proved that truths about himself and his party of thieves, criminals, and murderers. Hillary allowed a fellow Senator because she was a woman to be harassed as if she had killed four people with her bare hands in Benghazi. And wanted her to be jailed and not the mastermind behind the Benghazi attack. His profound hatred for the twice legally elected and beloved President Barack Obama is the source of much of his evil. Mitch before his soul I handed over to the demons in hell much of what he says he stands for will be discredited and disproved.

We all know that the older you get the worse of a person you become in general and it takes a huge effort to become a better person, ask the saintly among us. Mitch McConnell and many of the oldest jackasses voted in office are the worst human beings on the planet and they are leaders in the world.

Prophesy: North Korea beware of the one running your country who has committed a myriad of crimes against humanity against millions and killed hundreds of thousands of North Koreans. What will time that make of him in only a few short decades more? Will you survive that demon? And this same Prophesy goes out to the Russian Citizenry and especially the Filipino citizenry.

McConnell has supported lie after lie after lie after lie, and the diabolical result is that all the truths told about him sound like lies themselves and all of the lies he has told have been self revealing. The good people of Kentucky have done nothing to deserve the evil of this man except not perceive the evil of this man and his demon cohort. There is more than one demon he has courted.

This man is a repugnant human being at best. A pig in the proper truest sense of the word. He is a disgrace and doesn't deserve his job. It is not about winning all arguments to the exclusion of all other information it is about representation. And I asked every Kentuckian do you feel well represented? Do you have good health insurance for your whole life like he does? Do you have a pension and billionaire donors who will support you as he does? Do all of the women in Kentucky know that if you have a child and your lover does not want it that you can get an abortion plus a million dollars with no public rebuke? This is an indictment of his party that no one has the balls to openly defy him at the present moment. His colleagues are way more craven and scared of him than Trump and have forgotten that they are public

servants not armies of the damned.

And what will Democrats do to thwart him? **Call for an investigation into his**

multitudinous crimes? Oh yeah, those will do the trick, especially with Mitch McConnell

presiding over the Senate. I call on the truly good people of this country to take back the

Senate this fall of 2018, and take back our country. We the people deserve better, so much

better. Let the majority exercise true democratic reform and keep us from heading down a

path chosen by an evil few and their demons.

"Obviously, any foreign breach of our Cybersecurity measures is disturbing and I

strongly condemn any such efforts," McConnell said **in a statement that** he read to

reporters at a news conference at the US Capitol.

Strongly condemn, is this Kremlin prepared speech a joke? Will not the good souls of

Kentucky recall this joke of a human being? So that he can call his Kremlin handlers and tell

them the news that they do not want to hear. "The people of the United States of America

have rejected our evil plans which we have foisted upon them." That his demon Moloch will

have to take a beating from Satan because has been revealed.

We must remember that we are a liberal constitutional democracy founded by liberals

not conservatives! At the time of the American Revolution conservatives what would have

been know as Tories. They wanted to stay with the English crown. This treatise was completed on our countries birthday in 2018 and let us honor those liberals who gave us this wonderful form of government, of the people, by the people and for the people. Let us remind our radical conservative citizens that the Kremlin has a conservative constitutional democracy for them and they are certainly encouraged to join them but leave your beliefs about abortion, bibles, guns, businesses, protests against abortion or corruption, and opinions because they will not be welcome there. Ask Edward Snowden and see first hand how it is working out for him. He is quoted as publicly saying, "The Russian government is entirely corrupt." (2018) Will Vladimir had him over to Donald J. Trump?

Paul Ryan

House Speaker Paul Ryan is the biggest fraud in American politics who is leaving Congress after trying his best to destroy health insurance for millions and defraud the American people of the Social Security and Medicare that they had paid Trillions into for generations. Good riddance.

House Speaker Paul Ryan, named "Urka-Shiat-si-Ah" by his demon master "Legion", is announcing his retirement, Thank God! Today another prayer to God Almighty has been answered!!! He is the biggest phony in American political life during his time in Congress. Praise to Jesus Christ Son of the Living God he is going!

Prophesy: Never to return to national politics.

Paul Ryan had always wanted more for his constituents as a public servant. He has lusted after the power to improve the lives of the wealthy while reducing the living standards of the all others. He also craved a certain form of respectability that's led him to leave behind a staggering track record of broken promises, fake reforms, abandoning true government oversight for partisan bickering and pettiness. This is the hope for the future those who farm in the debauchery of Kremlin policies. Not so pretty sleeping with the enemy.

From his early days as an uninformed Social Security reformer whatever that is? To his intellectually dishonest period posturing as a deficit hawk who has signed more legislation as Speaker of the House to increase the deficit any any other previous speaker. To his re-branding as a person deeply concerned with poverty by his tax giveaways to the wealthiest and his niggardly scraps that he has temporarily thrown at the average person who voted him into office. Eventually, the con ran out, leaving Paul Ryan with little in the way of substantive accomplishments as he chose to cut and run before a midterm election that's shaping up to be a race between his party's deep unpopularity and the humongous resistance to the Donald J. Trump White House of lies.

Social Security Reform: The basic idea here was that George W. Bush's administration wanted to use the program's long-term fiscal deficit as a pretext to alter its fundamental structure away from a guarantee of a decent standard of living in retirement to one where individuals would be reliant on private investment accounts. Instead of paying back the American people for what previous Congresses had stolen from them because that would be the correct course of action.

Paul Ryan emerged as a player by sponsoring, along with then-Sen. John Sununu, another wrong headed morally corrupt plan not to pay the American people back but rather would create more generous private accounts having the deficit producing effects of adding 2.4 Trillion dollars to future generations. Now you get to see how he is shaping his future to be a deficit hawk, against himself and his party. Please remember that those living through the 1990's experienced a surplus and the Republicans were quick to squander it away because they stand for NOTHING! This brilliant scheme of Paul Ryan would as the Center on Budget and Policy Priorities foretold, "the plan would increase the national debt every year for at least the next 75 years."

This failure deeply hurt Paul Ryan as his feckless deep seated desire to sell out his own countrymen was not assuaged. The plan went nowhere because Bush found better ways of destroying our economy than had been done by any Republican White House occupant since Nixon. The only way that republicans get away with this nonsense is because American school systems are notoriously poor especially in history.

This serious life lesson did not stop Paul Ryan from branding himself a few years later as a deficit hawk. The key to the Republican public servants, Fox News, Sinclair Broadcasting, and Trump fake news is to announce that you are the opposite of what you are and that you say you do the opposite of what you truly do. A perfect example is Paul Ryan called the Tax cuts tax reform. He assumes that the American people are so profoundly stupid that they do not know that tax reform is deficit neutral and tax cuts add to the deficit. We elect public servants who have no respect for their constituents. Personally I do not let an issue go by without telling my duly elected officials what my opinion is and kick out of office those who do not follow the will of their constituents.

Paul Ryan's actual record in Congress, which had featured support for multiple rounds of budget-busting Bush tax cuts, Bush's deficit-financed 2003 Medicare bill, his wars, and his TARP bank bailout. But the new improved Paul Ryan now stands for nothing except giving huge tax breaks to the wealthiest of Americans who will never notice it. Keeping his mouth shut as the infestation in the White House makes racists and misogynistic comments. This is supposed to be the party of Lincoln? I am just kidding. This is the House Speaker who allowed on his watch illegal trade war started by the previously mentioned infestation and said and did nothing. Just watched as the Midwest took the brunt of the insane money losing proposition. This is all done by Donald J. Trump to weaken America. Sat back and watched as his fellow republican congressional clowns, Matt Gaetz "Urk-nnah-breenk-nah", Devin Nunez "Urka-breenk-tuvkla", and Jim Jordan "Urknah-ped-rost-hah", all under the power of Legion, attack and lie about the Department of Justice and the Federal Bureau of Investigation.

Paul Ryan much to the chagrin of the demons which surround him he fails at the things he did tries to do even their prodding him to remove the chaplain of the congress failed miserably. Paul Ryan's career ended in abject failure!

Donald J. Trump

This section of the Axis of Evil must start with a question to the American People. Why would you vote for a person who has never washed his own underwear or cooked himself a meal? What could such a person offer to the average American? Why would you not come out in droves to vote against a racist, misogynist, ignoramus, who promoted the idea that his detractors should be physically hurt by his supporters? What does this say about the supporters as well as those who did not vote? How do we support a democratic system where the popular vote can be overruled? Where are our patriots? Where are those who love our country? Where is our civility?

I want to take seriously the proposition that we have a lying, incompetent, immoral, and criminal president. We don't just have a rude president. We don't just have a lying president. We don't just have a racist, misogynist president. Such judgments have become commonplace and are shared by all members of or society even the most cynical and perverse Fox News personalities like Sean Hannity, "Urka-bu-shush-tah" as he is named by his demon Surgat.

Let us take this line of reasoning to its logical conclusion: We actually have an evil occupant of the White House. Every commentator even the most disciplined cannot describe the horror show that is the White House except in moral terms. In his first year in office, and particularly on foreign policy, Donald Trump has been a force for evil. I am arguing that he is personally an evil doer, not only does he think and act in an evil manner. He surrounds himself with evil doers. I am not speaking theologically. I do not believe that Trump sold his soul to the devil in exchange for wealth and worldly power. You cannot sell what you do not own. For all of us bringing the world to the edge of nuclear holocaust, destroying our relations with our allies and neighbors, destroying the planet for future generations, and inciting discord among your fellow citizens in the here and now are evil. And Donald J. Trump has shifted U.S. policy in these directions.

What is truly problematic is how many uneducated and foul thinking members of our own people agree with this monster. These evil souls had to be outed in some fashion. So called conservatives and white evangelicals, Trump's cheering section, despite all their nonsense about right and wrong. It's bad enough that they bent over backwards to rationalize Roy Moore's predatory conduct toward girls and Trump's serial adultery. The biggest problem is Donald J. Trump's attitude to the world as a whole.

For the past 70 years or so sober minded people have strategically focused on political and economic issues. It has been until modern day Tories who focus on fake culture wars which the Kremlin is quick to run its divide and conquer playbook against. Intolerance whether moral, legal, racial or political will always play into the hands of our enemies both human and demonic. Perhaps it's time for us to recapture the energy of the civil rights and women's rights movements? What is at root at the root of being an American is the moral strength that we have to offer because material wealth can and will be co-opted by evil just ask the Mercers about how that happens. We have a moral wealth that is not destructible unless we destroy it by doing no good.

To quote former Vice President Dick Cheney, someone who has had more than a passing acquaintance with the Dark Side, you don't negotiate with evil.

You defeat evil.

Fig. 15 Basilica of the National Shrine of the Immaculate Conception, Washington, DC
Representation of Our Lady of Vietnam.

True Winning

Winning at any price is thievery.

The legal path to the presidency of the United states of America is the Super Bowl Tuesday of all American democratic elections. But some of us who have watched presidential elections since before we understood its significance may find ourselves perplexed: What sort of human activity are we participating in or just are we just watching? Are we voting someone off of the island? I this a popularity contest to see who will be king and queen of a four year prom?

And who are these bigger than life men and women competing for our attention and our votes. If both candidates want what is best for all of us, then why do they not work together? Why would they throw mud and bile at one another if it is my vote they want? Why would I vote for someone who acts morally corrupt? If you smelt it you dealt it. That is if you are so familiar with the sins of another it is because you have done or are doing the very same sins. Why would I vote for someone who breaks the cardinal truth of my youth? If you have nothing good to say then do not say anything. Why would I vote for someone who breaks the cardinal rule of my adulthood, "If you are not part of the solution, THEN YOU ARE THE PROBLEM". Own it!

What the alpha candidate rarely reveals are the beta and gamma men and women behind the scenes. A laundry list of names and personalities that we will only come to know when they resign or quit their prestigious jobs. Or come to the public attention because of their inability to act civilly, legally or morally. The hopefully high but fair standards exhibited by the Alpha candidate will be followed by his / her army of devotees.

We are a long way from those heady days. We live in a world where the Alpha candidate is a nincompoop and exhibits the moral leadership of a reckless mobster. I do apologize for this comparison is an insult to mobsters everywhere. But one message has come through no matter what the final outcome of the Donald J. Trump conspiracy. He conspired with the Kremlin to win the presidency, and threatens to do more harm, if that is possible. No one is above the law even if you choose your own judges we all know what happens to mob bosses. Even McDonald's eating Donald J. Trump know what happens to them.

Donald your fate is assured and your ancestors nightly call to you, keeping you awake. I hear their screams in my visions and nightmares. I know and feel what happens to you and why you are so afraid.   Those nightmares and visages are horrific! That is what Melania sprinkles holy water around so as to defend herself and her child from your demons. You have only to ask God, the American people and the world for forgiveness and resign. Your demons will flee. Now we wait and see if your are smart enough to heed this prophetic treatise.

Life is not a game or a reality show. Being a leader means you have to lead and by both your word and example. Else you are just playing a very expensive game and all games have winners and losers.

Enjoy the game.

Chapter 13

Fig. 16 Basilica of the National Shrine of the Immaculate Conception, Washington, DC
Representation of Our Lady of Sorrows.

Apostasy

Apostasy the abandonment or renunciation of a religious or political belief.

Ivanka Trump is an apostate from Christianity. She formally apostatized, that is, she renounced her baptism and denied that Our Lord and Savior Jesus Christ is God Incarnate who died for the sins of the world. So that she could marry her husband, Jared Kushner.

Kushner is now one of Trump's senior advisers and is even in charge of all foreign relations with his deep state experience in all things criminal, as he was home schooled. Jared Kushner is a practicing Talmudic Jew. So, Ivanka had to formally renounce Jesus Christ Our Lord and Savior in order to marry Kushner. They are now raising their children as "observant" Talmudic Jews.

Ivanka Trump's children obviously are not baptized. That means three of Donald Trump's grandchildren are not baptized. And his apostate daughter and son-in-law who are responsible for this horror are his two top senior advisers.

Tell me again about Donald Trump's deep Christian faith.

Chapter 14

Fig. 17 Basilica of the National Shrine of the Immaculate Conception, Washington, DC
Representation of the Gospel Writer Saint Mark.

Judas

(Judas famous for betraying Jesus Christ Son of the Living God.)

Jesus commanded his followers to be distinct from their Jewish brethren. He commanded them to be perfect as his Heavenly Father is perfect. He did not command that they be human slavers, racists, misogynists, antisemites or homophobes. He does not nor did it ever occur to his followers to be this way. Though many claim to be his followers they exercise these human failings and they claim to do it in His name. What a kiss of betrayal! Love God with your whole heart mind body and soul. Love your neighbor as yourself. This is what he commanded. To the extent that your spiritual, business, political and moral leaders stray from these commands as well as ignore the ten commandments. They also betray Jesus with a kiss of Judas.

They should be shunned as betrayers of Jesus. The kiss given to a baby on a political campaign while making sure that her future is stolen by denying basic human necessities such as health care. This is the kiss of betrayal. Kissing your gay child while you stomp on the rights of other gay children of God is a kiss of betrayal. Kissing your mother, sister, female cousin or wife and believing that she is not worth being treated fairly in business, or pay or value is the Judas kiss of betrayal. Giving the kiss of peace at church to your neighbor who you believe is not your neighbor and that he should return to whatever place other than your neighborhood. This is the kiss of betrayal of Judas.

John the beloved Apostle laid his head on the breast of Jesus. There is no more intimate a scene among the time that Jesus was with His Apostles than this and no more of a holy scene than this. This is what we all desire who are true lovers of Jesus. The kiss of Judas was also intimate and it is what we give to Jesus with our betrayals. We can only do our best by loving our neighbor as ourselves and by loving all humans both the born and the unborn. Many who profess to love the unborn treat the born like crap. This is another kiss of betrayal.

Chapter 15

SCA
PERPCTVA
SCA
FELICITAS
ALIUS ERIT
PATIETR pro
ET EGO pro
me qui
me qua
no pasura
sum·

Fig. 18 Basilica of the National Shrine of the Immaculate Conception, Washington, DC
Representation of Saints Perpetua and Felicity.

Dossier

The label for this document is Republican Candidate Donald J. Trump's activities in Russia and compromising relationship with the Kremlin.

Four Point Summary:

I. Russian regime has been cultivating, supporting and assisting Donald J. Trump for at LEAST 5 years. Their aim which has been endorsed by Vladimir Putin has been to encourage splits and divisions in Western Alliances, (EU, NATO, NAFTA, TPP etc).

II. Donald J. Trump and his inner circle have accepted a regular flow of intelligence from the Kremlin, (which has not stopped to this very day), including on his Democratic and Republican political rivals.

III. Former top Russian intelligence officer claims FSB has compromised Donald J. Trump through his activities in Moscow sufficiently to be able to blackmail him. According to several knowledgeable sources, his conduct in Moscow has included perverted sexual acts which have been arranged / monitored by the FSB.

IV. A dossier of compromising material on Hillary Clinton has been collated by the Russian Intelligence Services over many years and mainly comprises bugged conversations she had on various visits in Russia and intercepted phone calls rather than any embarrassing conduct. The Dossier is controlled by Kremlin spokesman, Peskov, directly on Putin's orders. However it has not as yet been distributed abroad, including to Donald J. Trump. Russian intentions for its deployment are still unclear.

Points for Donald Trump to hand to his Kremlin handler Vladimir Putin in his upcoming meeting in Helsinki.

1. Sow seeds of discord with in the United States of America an especially within G7 and NATO. Offer European countries to leave the EU. Done!

2. Beat Hillary Clinton by any means necessary in the 2016 election. Done!

3. Spy on G7 member states granting Kremlin phone updates which would be told to the world by the Kremlin to stymie the Free Western Press. Done!

4. Send over Western visitors to have them bugged so that they will help the Kremlin understand and thwart FBI investigations which still befuddle the Kremlin. Failed!

   - As much as the clowns on Capital Hill like Jim Jordan, Trey Gowdy, Devin Nunes, Sean Hannity and the Trump buffoons have tried to give the Russians all of the Intel they can on the FBI's methods the courts have kept them at bay although it is my hunch that Jeff Sessions will give away those secrets to his Russian handlers.

5. Complete agreement to collusion to hack the DNC as well as exchange information back and forth using Paul Manafort. Done!

6. Many wonder why the Illegitimate occupant of the White House denies his own intelligence groups that is because he still relies on the Kremlin's Intelligence

officers who have all been invited to the US even though one is under Sanctions. Ask fat boy Pompeo about that...

7. Show complete trust in Wikileaks. Done!

8. Heap huge amounts of fake negative talk about Barack Obama who Putin fears and hates. Done!

9. Sideline the Ukraine issues for the Republicans and take the Kremlin's talking points that Crimea belongs to the Russians. Done!

10. Kremlin's responsibilities was to keep Trump flush with cash and prostitutes. Done!

11. Carter Page recruited as a spy have the clowns on capital hill use him to get copies of FISA records and report to his Kremlin handlers on how the FBI found out about him. Done!

12. Kremlin fears grow as DNC hacked information becomes public and they contact the campaign to cool things down while Trump co conspirators tell the Kremlin that they will ratchet up Hillary conspiracy tales to befuddle the news cycle. Paul Manafort reports into his Kremlin handler the an oligarch Deripaska. Done!

13. Donald J. Trump was to constantly deny the Kremlin's involvement in the attack against the U.S.A. and to back him up would be the Russian bots used before, during and forever after. Done!

14. As the Kremlin believed that sanctions against the oligarchs would divide them against each other, which will happen when Vladimir Putin dies. They believed that their chaos caused in the Divided States of Trumperica was much stronger and

longer lasting. Prophesy: Russia will split into many different countries during a

100-year of civil war and will never recover as a world power.

Donald J. Trump supported by the Kremlin because he was seen as a divisive, anti-

establishment candidate who would shake up current international status quo in Russia's

favor. Donald J. Trump was seen also as divisive in disrupting the whole US political

system especially with his two incompetent henchmen little Paul and tiny Mitch. He was

also a businessman who would help them get oil to $100 a barrel which is what they need

for cash.

The ending thought to this is fight, laugh and love with each other. The aforementioned

clowns in this treatise for the most part will not amend their evil ways are going on the first

class non-stop trip to hell. And in all honesty Thanks be to God for that justice. Fight the

Russian threat by avoiding using oil and gas. That is the life blood which keeps the

Kremlin afloat until we end this planet through global warming.

Or we stop them in their tracks by going green. The day that Donald J. Trump, (aka ding

dong), pulled us out of the Paris Accord I got rid of my vehicle. There are many ways to

stop them. Plastic bags are made from petroleum products. The fewer dollars we spend

on petroleum products gives our home (the earth) and ourselves a chance to survive and

leaves Kremlin penniless. May God Bless You!

The End

Fig. 19 Basilica of the National Shrine of the Immaculate Conception, Washington, DC
Representation Over the archway at the northeast entrance of the Basilica.